HACK YOUR HIRING

HACK YOUR
HIRING

THE TACTICAL PLAYBOOK
TO FIND, EVALUATE, AND
HIRE A+ TALENT

SHAUN P. MARTIN

HACK YOUR HIRING

THE TACTICAL PLAYBOOK TO FIND, EVALUATE, AND HIRE A+ TALENT

© 2018 **SHAUN P. MARTIN**

ISBN: 978-1-79288-972-1 Paperback

Independently Published by Rebase LLC
Austin, TX 78704
https://rebase.cc

DEDICATION

To my parents, Sue and Steve, who always challenge me to become the best version of myself.

And to every mentor, manager & coach who saw potential in me.

Thank you. Without you, none of this would be possible.

CONTENTS

PREFACE

I want to congratulate you for committing to upgrade your efforts in building a winning team.

Hiring can be extremely frustrating and feel a bit like a black box sometimes. The good news is that you absolutely do NOT need a ton of resources when you can be resourceful.

As every leader & every company face different hiring challenges, the strategies that appeal to you, and the ones you decide to implement, will differ for everyone. Before you dive in, I want to make one simple recommendation:

You're going to find a lot of ideas you want to try out, and by all means I want you to achieve the success you deserve. However, it will be best to exercise a little restraint and try to yourself to only implementing one or two of these strategies at a time.

Why only one or two?

Well, it's a best practice I learned in my engineering career, and something all scientific disciplines understand. It's part of the scientific method and critical for testing the effectiveness of a new experiment: You have to limit the variables in any experiment if you want to be able to really understand what's successful for you.

For example, let's say I constantly felt tired and sluggish, and I wanted to make some changes in my diet to see if it helped. So, I suddenly quit consuming dairy AND red meat AND pasta, and within just a few weeks I start feeling better.

While the result is great, I have no idea which ONE was potentially causing my health issues, or even if it was TWO or ALL THREE. Maybe I gave up red meat for no reason (a personal nightmare for me). Does that make sense?

Admittedly, often times these do work best in combination with others, so you absolutely can combine them. Just keep in mind, then, that it's only the effectiveness of that combination you can then understand.

But that's enough from me. I wish you nothing but good fortune on your journey to recruiting mastery!

Cheers!

Shaun P. Martin

INTRODUCTION

When I speak with potential customers and consulting clients about their hiring challenges, the primary issues that prevent them from hiring A+ Talent quickly, reliably, and repeatedly vary widely from company to company.

However, their problems always seem to fall into one or two of the categories I call the Components of High-Performance Hiring. And while companies use the the components differently, every employer relies on these components to add new people to their organization. If you haven't gotten your free copy of the 5 Components of High-Performance Hiring Cheatsheet, I highly recommend you do so at *hack-your-hiring.com/5-components-cheatsheet*.

With almost every company I've worked with, there are things that are broken in several components. Yet without fail, once an Employer is able to diagnose which of these components is the most broken, we're able to focus, execute, and fix what's broken.

WHAT THIS BOOK WILL AND WILL NOT DO FOR YOU

This book is going to show you all the Components involved in your recruiting practices, and it will introduce you to some new terms and concepts you may not already be familiar with.

It's going to show you new & creative ways to improve the health of your recruiting practices so that you can find, evaluate and hire A-Players in any job market more quickly, confidently and reliably. It's going to show you what to do, but it will not do the work for you. No book, no resource is nearly as valuable as the action you take because of it. How you implement these strategies, who you involve, the quality of your effort, is completely up to you.

I designed this book to be a companion reference manual to your efforts in building a team that wins by shepherding job-seekers through a Candidate Experience that rocks.

Keep This Book On Your Desktop

As job market and economic conditions change, so do the challenges you face in hiring A-Players. When there's low unemployment and easy access to cheap capital, as is the case at the time of publishing, you face a candidate-driven market where sourcing A+ Talent is your biggest challenge.

But if a few companies go belly-up or experience massive layoffs tomorrow, you could find yourself with hundreds or thousands of new applicants, and now screening and evaluating more effectively becomes your priority.

My goal is that this will become a daily or weekly reference for you as you are continuing to build and grow your team.

HOW TO GET THE MOST OUT OF THIS BOOK

While you could absolutely read this cover-to-cover, I recommend you focus on

A) The Components or Stages where you are weakest, or

B) The Components where creating a measured improvement will provide the greatest overall impact.

Each Strategy contains the following ingredients:

➢ **Instructions:** The first section of each strategy contains a simple set of instructions on what to do to apply the strategy. While there are certainly steps you can add to supplement the strategy and make it your own, this will be your baseline.

➢ **Why It Works:** The philosophy, the thinking and reasoning behind the strategy. It also references research and behavioral factors that back-up the strategy's effectiveness. Understanding this will go a long way in helping you apply the strategy in the way that's most successful for your unique situation.

➤ **Achievements Unlocked:** Much like a strategy book for a video game (my childhood was a key inspiration for creating this book) the final section explains exactly what you will accomplish and how your recruiting practices will improve through executing the strategy.

KEY CONCEPTS:
THE CHARACTERS, STAGES & ELEMENTS

A Recruiting process is kinda like a video game, like Super Mario Bros. Every game is different, though they also share similarities. In every game, there are Characters, Stages, and Elements.

THE CHARACTERS

Just as Mario is not the only character in Super Mario Bros, there are a host of different characters in the recruiting process. Every person you interact with, everyone who is affected by your actions both directly and indirectly, plays a Character in the game.

In fact, the person you want to hire actually changes Character slightly as she's bookd through the recruiting process. It's kinda like how Mario can be Tiny Mario, Big Mario, Fireball Mario or Invincible Mario. Same mustached plumber, slightly different character.

Below are the primary characters in the Recruiting game:

➤ **Hiring Manager:** The person ultimately responsible for making a hiring decision. Typically also the person defining a role, the job's skill requirements. A new hire will report to this person either directly or a few levels up.

➢ **Recruiter:** The person(s) staffed by your company, either as an employee or contractor, who contacts Prospects and operates the mechanics of the recruiting process. Recruiters also typically make the physical offer to a candidate. This person could have a variety of job titles, such as Recruiting Coordinator, Operations Manager, or HR Generalist.

➢ **Recruiting Agency / Staffing Company:** These terms are used interchangeably in this book. This includes any organization or individual you are contracted with that you pay to send you pre-qualified candidates who are interested in the job.

➢ **Job-Seeker:** Anyone considering switching to a new opportunity. This includes people actively applying for your role and passive prospects who would be open to a new opportunity.

➢ **Prospect:** Someone who may be qualified for the job but has not yet shown explicit interest in being considered.

➢ **Applicant:** A person who wants to be considered for the job and has provided a CV or Résumé.

➢ **Candidate:** An Applicant who "on paper" meets at least the minimum requirements of the role. Once someone enters the Screening and Evaluating stages, she is a Candidate until she is rejected, she removes herself from considering, or she accepts an offer.

THE STAGES

In Mario's World (see what I did there?) he starts at the First Stage, and progresses through a series of increasingly challenging stages until the game is over.

Whether he completes every stage, loses all his lives, or you decide to quit the game, a collection of characters will be present and participating in each stage. Obviously, the collection of characters who participate in each stage are different.

In Recruiting, stages generally map to the components of high-performance hiring.

➢ **Profile:** The stage in which the Hiring Manager, Recruiter and Sourcing Partners define exactly who and what you're looking for in an ideal new hire.

➢ **Sourcing:** Once you've painted a clear picture of your ideal hire with a Position Profile, this is the stage where you fill your bucket with interested applicants using a variety of methods.

➢ **Screening:** The point at which, given a pool of applicants, you separate the signal from the noise and transform qualified applicants into candidates.

➢ **Evaluating:** Candidates who pass your Screening methods are now in the Evaluating stage, where the employing company engages the candidate for one or more interviews to determine if she is an accurate reflection of her résumé and if she is a fit for the position, team and company.

➢ **Closing:** Once a decision has been reached that the employer wants to hire a candidate, an offer is composed and every effort is made to secure her as your newest team member.

THE ELEMENTS

In any process, there are intangible concepts we will refer to here as Elements. A good example of an element in Mario is the timer at the top of the screen, counting down and letting the player know how much time they have to complete the stage.

➢ **Candidate Experience:** The quality of the time spent from start-to-finish as viewed through the eyes of a candidate, no matter where the end is for her.

➢ **Cycle Time:** The amount of time it takes from the start of a process to a clearly defined end. For example, overall cycle time is the time that elapses from the time a Job-Seeker applies until she accepts an offer, and evaluating cycle time is the amount of time that elapses between when you advance a candidate to the evaluating stage and when you complete your evaluation and make a hire/no-hire decision.

➢ **Employer Brand:** The reputation of your organization in regards to how it recruits, onboards, develops and generally values its employees.

➢ **Time-to-Hire:** The time that elapses between opening a position and filling it.

PART ONE

PROFILE

Defining an open position does not start with a Job Description. Most job descriptions are overly vague where it matters, and oddly specific where it doesn't.

Rarely do they clearly articulate the parameters for success in the role.

Defining an open position begins with a clear picture and understanding of what determines *success* in the role.

A-Players want to be successful. They want to overcome Obstacles and produce the Outputs achieve clearly-articulated Outcomes.

The following Strategies will help you clearly understand and articulate the exact skills, strengths and characteristics exemplified by The Profile of an A-Player, making every other step in the Recruiting process more easy and straightforward.

USE THE 4 Os FRAMEWORK TO ATTRACT A+ TALENT

Rather than composing a Job Description from a list of Activities and Skills, answer the following 4 questions to paint a clear picture of what success in this position looks like.

1. What are some of the Outcomes the person in this role will produce for the company / your customers / her teammates / herself? In other words, what types of impact will she have on their lives?

2. What are a few of the Outputs the person in this role will produce, contribute to, or oversee that you believe will achieve those Outcomes?

3. What Obstacles is she likely to encounter in efforts to produce the Outputs and achieve the Outcomes? Every person, no matter what her job, encounters obstacles to performing her duties, every week, without fail.

4. What are the competencies, technical skills, and intangible strengths she would need to exhibit in over to Overcome the biggest Obstacles, produce the Outputs, and achieve the Outcomes?

Let me ask you a question: Is it possible for a Candidate to have exactly the Expertise you're seeking and be able to perform every Activity expected of them ... and still fail in a role?

Of course it is.

By defining what success looks like for a particular position, you not only identify more intangible strengths and relevant experience, but you have built a foundation of expectations that will be far more appealing to the Achiever-mindset that is prevalent in all A-Players.

🏆 ACHIEVEMENTS UNLOCKED

➢ Clarify Understanding of Success In This Role
➢ Improve Prospect Engagement
➢ Establish Foundation for
   ○ Identifying Relevant Experience
   ○ Screening Applicants
   ○ Evaluating Candidates
   ○ Conducting Performance Reviews

SOURCE STRENGTHS & SKILLS FROM COLLEAGUES

Reach out to current teammates who you'd consider an A-Player with experience in a position similar to your open role.

Ask each teammate plainly about

> What *Outputs* and *Outcomes* he's most proud of contributing to or creating

> What *Obstacles* he's faced in his career

> What they believe contributed to his success in *Overcoming* those obstacles, from when he first started to his ability to grow and flourish in the role.

Every Job and every Candidate is going to be unique in some fashion. However, no Job is so unique that it's without ample comparative examples. By compiling a list of obstacles, strengths, and skills from the experience of others you trust, you start building a sort of composite avatar of your ideal Candidate.

ACHIEVEMENTS UNLOCKED

- ➤ Clarify Understanding of Success In This Role
- ➤ Establish Foundation to
  - ○ Identify Relevant Experience
  - ○ Screen Applicants
  - ○ Evaluate Candidates
  - ○ Conduct Performance Reviews

COMPLETE THE 4 OS EXERCISE WITH FORMER COLLEAGUES

1. Reach out to a former A+ employee who held a position similar to the one you're currently trying to fill. Offer to meet over lunch or a drink, if necessary.
2. Explain to him that he's someone you admire for his achievements and contributions and that you would like to find out what made him successful so that you can add someone like him to your team now.
3. When you meet, ask him about the Outcomes he feels he accomplished during his time. Be diligent about ensuring these are Outcomes and not just Outputs.
4. Once you have an acceptable list of significant Outcomes, inquire as to what Outputs he produced, contributed to, oversaw and/or managed that contributed to achieving the Outcomes.
5. For each Output, ask him to recall every Obstacle that arose along the way.
6. Lastly, ask him what enabled he and the team to overcome those Obstacles, specifically the strengths & abilities he exhibited.

While your current openings are going to differ in some ways from the job performed by former employees and your colleagues at previous companies, they're also going to share a ton of similarities.

Instead of having to speculate or outright guess about what constitutes the Profile of an A-Player, why not ask one?

Your former colleague will be flattered that you think highly of him and want his advice, and they get an opportunity to talk about his successes. It's a win for everyone.

🏆 ACHIEVEMENTS UNLOCKED

➤ Shorten Time to Complete Position Profile

GRADE EXPERTISE IN USEFUL TERMS

For each technical skill and intangible strength, grade the level of expertise using a method that clearly describes the ideal candidate's level of competency & expertise.

Useful Frameworks to reference include:

- Four Stages of Competence$_1$
- National Institute of Health's Competencies Proficiency Scale$_2$
- Dreyfus Model of Skill Acquisition$_3$
- Bloom's Taxonomy$_4$

The conventional method of conveying desired levels of expertise was born from the requirement of formal education (2-year / 4-year degree), and in most cases it has outlived its usefulness.

As an increasing percentage of the workforce becomes knowledge workers, the search for expertise hinges on the ability to find candidates who have actually grown and developed a level of expertise or mastery in various skills.

Unfortunately, spending years exercising a particular skill in no way guarantees that a worker increased her expertise in that skill.

Isn't it true that someone who's been driving a car for 10 years could still be a poor driver? Or that someone with a good teacher + some natural talent could be an excellent driver in his first few years behind the wheel?

Here's a personal example: At the time I'm writing this, I am 36 years old. I have been using MS Excel and other spreadsheet software since the age of 10. The claim could be made, then, that I have 26 years of Excel experience, yet I will be the first person to admit that I am far from a Excel/Spreadsheet Expert.

Using a commonly-understand and explicit grading scale to describe levels of expertise is the best way to communicate -- both internally and externally -- what levels of proficiency are required to succeed in a particular role.

🏆 **ACHIEVEMENTS UNLOCKED**

➢ Increase Understanding of Desired Expertise
➢ Objective Measurement of Skills to Share with Recruiters & Sourcing Partners

FORCE-RANK DESIRED SKILLS

In addition to more clearly defining desired levels of Expertise for a role, classify the importance of a candidate exhibiting each skill to the desired level of Expertise. This can be as simple as classifying a skill as "Must-Have" / "Should-Have" / "Nice-to-Have", or you could use a more complex ordering mechanism.

There is no position on earth where every desired competency is equally critical to achieving success in the role. Yet, Job Descriptions nearly always provide a list of skills that appear to be of equal importance (and are usually all required).

This can deter many otherwise-qualified job-seekers, while also inviting applications from unqualified candidates who don't have a clear sense of which areas truly require a level of expertise vs those where familiarity or basic competence are acceptable.

It's also important to recognize that an Applicant's expertise in a particular area is constantly changing and would continue to change if they came to work for you. The Résumé they submit is a mere snapshot of a moment in time. If there are skills where "Expert" would be nice but "Intermediate" is Critical, it's important to call this out.

A Hiring Manager who struggles to fill urgent roles almost always struggles precisely because he's not explicitly clear -- with himself and with others -- which skills and skill-levels are critical, important, desirable, or simply a nice bonus.

 ACHIEVEMENTS UNLOCKED

➢ Increase Flexibility in Evaluating Candidate Strength
➢ Increase Quality Applicant Volume
➢ Improve Screening Quality

SHARE YOUR PROFILE WITH SOURCING PARTNERS

Once you've finalized the Position Profile for an open role, share it with recruiters, staffing companies, your company's leadership, employees, etc.

Recruiting Agencies, staff Recruiters, Hiring Managers, Employees, Candidates … EVERYONE is so used to receiving bland, cold, corporate job descriptions & being asked to send quality candidates your way.

While creating a Position Profile doesn't exempt you from posting a more formal Job Ad to various Job Boards, providing your trusted partners this clear picture of what an A-Player looks like will be a pleasant & refreshing change from what they're used to seeing.

They're not only more likely to not only review it, they're more likely to examine it in great detail compared to a typical bland Job Description.

🏆 ACHIEVEMENTS UNLOCKED

- ➤ Increase Understanding of Desired Expertise
- ➤ Increase Applicant Quality
- ➤ Increase Quality Applicant Volume

PART TWO

SOURCING

Once you've painted a clear picture with a Position Profile, you can begin to ramp up and expand your sourcing efforts.

Sourcing is kinda like prospecting for customers, where in this scenario the customer is your A+ Talent. In your business, some customers discover *you*, through word-of-mouth, marketing or other efforts. Other customers are referred by friends or family. Still others only become your customer after you contact them directly.

There are literally hundreds of ways to acquire, cultivate and mature leads on potential candidates, and each way comes with its own associated cost.

That cost could be a fixed dollar amount, an investment of your time, employing dedicated staff, or some combination of all of these.

The Strategies contained in this section cover a wide range of effective Sourcing sub-categories, including Direct Outreach, Marketing, Employer Branding and Referrals.

SHARE SALARY UP-FRONT

Whether it's posted with your position description on job boards, or you keep it handy when having initial conversations with potential candidates, be transparent in letting them know what the salary range is for the role, as well as additional benefits the company offers (both material & intangible).

Compensation is consistently rated as one the top 3 reasons people decide to look for new opportunities. HIRED reports that 62% of candidates said a primary reason they'll engage with a company is when they get the salary range up-front.[5]

By sharing compensation details (salary, benefits, perks) early in the process, job-seekers will be able to decide if the salary range is aligned with their expectations.

Employers who go out of their way to obscure salary set themselves up for failure from the start, as they waste time evaluating candidates they can't afford. And since platforms like Glassdoor allow current & former employees to submit their salary information that will then be shared publicly, why try to hide it?

🏆 **ACHIEVEMENTS UNLOCKED**

➢ Build Job-Seeker/Employer Trust
➢ Allow Candidates With Differing Salary Expectations to Filter Themselves Out

---

SEND PROSPECTS A FREE GIFT

Empower Recruiters, Recruiting Researchers, & Recruiting Coordinators to send something of value to passive talent to get her engaged in the recruiting process. It can be something as simple as a link to an interesting article, video or product related to her discipline or area of expertise.

A-Players are already gun-shy when it comes to recruiting outreach, and it's not surprising as to why. Most Managers and Recruiters initiate outreach the complete wrong way: By focusing on themselves. This "Look at me and my great opportunity" approach is a big turn-off to an uber-talented person who gets hassled about new opportunities on a weekly or even daily basis.

The gift you send does not need to be expensive or even have any material cost, as long as it provides value.

In addition to breaking the pattern of bad behavior and thus immediately getting her attention, you may trigger a concept known as The Reciprocity Principle. The Reciprocity Principle is a well-documented principle of persuasion. Simply put, people are obliged to give back to others when they receive a gift or service first to ensure the interaction is balanced

ACHIEVEMENTS UNLOCKED

➤ Increase Prospect Engagement Rates

➤ Improve Employer Brand Quality

➤ Trigger the Reciprocity Principle

SEND A PERSONALIZED MESSAGE

When initiating Outbound contact with a Prospect, reference specific details about her work history, current role or interests. Ask a targeted question about one of these areas that will entice her to reply.

Recruiters & Hiring Managers have a tendency to play the numbers game when it comes to candidate outreach, relying on templates and form letters for the bulk of their communication. In a candidate-driven market, the key to grabbing an A-Player's attention is to make her feel special, like she's not just another number. If you can convey to her that you did your homework and that you want to learn more about her unique experiences & interests, she's far more likely to engage.

🏆 ACHIEVEMENTS UNLOCKED

➤ Improve Prospect Engagement
➤ Improve Employer Brand Quality

KEEP OUTREACH FUN AND LIGHT

Initiate contact with an attractive prospect with a congratulatory message as if she's just been offered your open position.

"Congratulations, Stephanie! I'm excited to offer you the position of Senior Engineer! The team loved you!

... Ok, so admittedly you'd have to go through the evaluation process first, but just think, Stephanie: I could be sending you a message just like this in just a few weeks. You could be just days from an exciting new opportunity! Nothing would make me happier ..."

In a job market where employers are doing nothing new or creative in terms of candidate outreach, practically anything that is fun, playful or creative is going to get a candidate's attention. There are hundreds of different ways to connect with prospects in a way that expresses personality. And in an industry that historically has a terrible reputation as being cold, impersonal & corporate, the amount of effort required to differentiate yourself is minimal.

🏆 ACHIEVEMENTS UNLOCKED

- ➤ Increase Prospect Engagement
- ➤ Improve Employer Brand Quality

INVITE PROSPECTS TO COMPANY EVENTS

When your company is having an event, be it community service, hiring events, or simply hosting a meetup, invite the prospects you've reached out to and connected with on a particular role.

ACHIEVEMENTS UNLOCKED, strengthens the relationship between a prospect and your company, makes them less likely to look for a job elsewhere.

Job Seekers want to work for a great company as well as work in a great opportunity. You need to humanize your company in order to appeal to a plus talent.

Inviting a prospect to simply hang out with her potential future coworkers allows them to get to know everyone and get a clearer picture in her mind of what it might be like to actually come and work with you.

🏆 ACHIEVEMENTS UNLOCKED

- ➢ Allow Prospects to interact with your team in a low pressure environment
- ➢ Strengthen the relationship between a prospect and your company
- ➢ Convert curious Prospects into engaged Candidates

FOCUS ON THEIR INTERESTS OVER YOURS

When Sourcing passive candidates, spend the majority of the time asking about their current challenges and career goals, and then genuinely listening to their responses.

Everyone loves talking about their favorite subject: Themselves. By asking simple, targeted questions about a job-seeker's current & desired career conditions, you get them to open up and connect with you. Now that you've established a genuine connection, she's more likely to become and stay engaged in your recruiting process.

NOTE: This is a great strategy for outbound sourcing, when candidates haven't yet indicated interest in your or your opportunity. It can, however, also be useful with those who have already applied for the role.

🏆 **ACHIEVEMENTS UNLOCKED**

➢ Increase Prospect Engagement
➢ Determine whether Employer needs align with where a Job-Seeker wants to grow in her career

---

TARGET CANDIDATES WHO KNOW A COLLEAGUE

When sourcing leads for recruiting outreach, target candidates who are connected on Facebook/LinkedIn/etc. to a current member of your staff.

In *HIRED's 2018 Employer Brand Survey*, 45% of candidates said a primary reason they'll engage with a company is if a friend or former colleague works there[6t]. So whether your colleagues put in the effort to provide referrals or not, it should not deter you from focusing your efforts on people they know and/or have worked with previously.

🏆 *ACHIEVEMENTS UNLOCKED*

➢ Increase Prospect Engagement
➢ Determine whether Employer needs align with where a Job-Seeker wants to grow in her career

---

REFINE AND PRACTICE YOUR PITCH

If you have a well-crafted & proven value proposition to sell to prospects, continually refine and practice the pitch. Practice it in the mirror, or record yourself delivering the pitch, or try it out with colleagues and get feedback. Practice the pitch until it becomes second nature.

Outbound Sourcing is 100% a sales discipline, and the quickest way to kill a Prospect's interest is a lack of confidence in the message you're delivering. You need to be able to confidently persuade a "cold" Prospect in order to convert them from a Prospect into an engaged Candidate.

Tweaking, refining and practicing your pitch grants you the confidence needed to convince prospects, whether it's by e-mail, phone or in-person.

🏆 *ACHIEVEMENTS UNLOCKED*

➢ Clarify Company Culture
➢ Improve Employer Brand Message
➢ Increase Prospect engagement rate

OFFER A REFERRAL INCENTIVE TO EMPLOYEES

Provide cash, gifts, equity etc. to Employees who refer a candidate who is successfully hired (typically after 30/60/90 days).

Assuming you've been hiring highly-talented people, they are your most reliable source of other highly-talented people. A-Players want to work with A-Players and they prefer to work with a known quantity, AKA people they've enjoyed working with in the past.

When you employ multiple people who've successfully worked well together in the past, you eliminate or reduce their need to learn how to work well with their new teammate(s).

🏆 ACHIEVEMENTS UNLOCKED

- ➢ Make Employees feel like a valued part of company growth
- ➢ Shorten Overall Cycle Time
- ➢ Reduce Sourcing Time Commitment for Recruiters & Hiring Managers
- ➢ Improve overall team performance

ASK FOR REFERRALS DURING ONBOARDING

When onboarding a new A-Player, ask her, "Who are the most talented people you know?" Make the question position- & discipline-agnostic, as you never know what the company may need to hire in the future.

An Employee Referral Program is a fantastic tool for sourcing A+ Talent, and Employers universally cite "Current Employees" as one of their best sources of quality candidates. That said, one of the challenges of building an effective Employee Referral Program is that Employees who've been working with you for longer periods of time may not have a strong network of A+ Talent extending outside your organization.

The A-Players you just hired don't have this limitation. Almost everyone in their network is from outside your organization, so strike while the iron's hot and build a list of highly-talented people you can reach out to.

🏆 ACHIEVEMENTS UNLOCKED

➢ Show New Employees you value & trust their opinions
➢ Shorten Overall Cycle Time
➢ Reduce Sourcing time commitment for Recruiters & Hiring Managers
➢ Shorten team "forming" period

ASK ACTIVE CANDIDATES FOR REFERRALS

When candidates are actively engaged in your process, ask them about the most talented people they know and have worked with, either at their current job or at a previous company. Tell them they could receive a referral reward if you end up hiring one of their referrals.

Just because a candidate is engaged in your evaluation process doesn't mean that she's going to end up being a fit. They could not be what you're seeking for a variety of reasons. That doesn't mean you should discount them as a resource for expanding your network of a plus talent.

This can work even if a candidate ends up rejecting your offer. If she's made it far enough in your evaluation process, then she's doing something right and should be viewed as a potentially viable source to find A+ Talent. Whether or not the lead she gave you turns into a hire, you've increased the chances that she'll engage with you in the future.

🏆 ACHIEVEMENTS UNLOCKED

- ➤ Show Candidates You Value Their Judgment
- ➤ Shorten Overall Cycle Time
- ➤ Reduce Sourcing Time Commitment for Recruiters & Hiring Managers

ASK FORMER EMPLOYEES FOR REFERRALS

Build an "Alumni Network" of former Employees, and connect with them regularly through email, social media or events. Ask them about the most talented people they've met or worked with.

Extending your Referral efforts to former Employees provides yet another valuable source of talented people that are "pre-vetted" by a trusted source.

People who left your company on good terms are likely to look back on their time with the company fondly, and they're more likely to be willing to contribute to your continued success.

ACHIEVEMENTS UNLOCKED

➢ Show former Employees You Value Their Time At Your Company & Their Judgment
➢ Show current Employees you'll respect and value them even after they've moved on to other opportunities
➢ Shorten Overall Cycle Time
➢ Reduce Sourcing Time Commitment for Recruiters & Hiring Managers

ENLIST TRUSTED CUSTOMERS, CLIENTS & PARTNERS IN A REFERRAL PROGRAM

In conversations with important customers, clients, vendors & partners, talk about your current initiatives or hiring needs and ask them about the A+ Talent they know or have met. Reward successful referrals with a gift of some sort (cash, gift cards, special offers/discounts).

Business Success in the Information Age relies heavily on cultivating strong relationships. What bigger compliment could a customer, client or partner receive than knowing you trust his judgment on the talent you might want to add to your team?

People who do repeat business with your company are, by nature of that relationship, invested in your success too. Rewarding them for the help they provide in finding talent simply strengthens this mutually-beneficial relationship.

ACHIEVEMENTS UNLOCKED

- ➢ Show business partners you value their input and believe they can contribute as much to your success as you do to theirs
- ➢ Shorten Overall Cycle Time
- ➢ Reduce Sourcing time commitment for Recruiters & Hiring Managers
- ➢ Strengthen business-critical relationships

RUN A PUBLIC TALENT REFERRAL CONTEST

Announce to your company's social media followers & fans that you are looking for A+ Talent in [insert role] and that anyone who refers a successful hire will receive a modest reward, in the form of a Gift Card or something similar.

People follow your company on social media because they feel they have some type of connection with you. If you can

1. Paint them a clear, specific picture of what your A-Player Profile looks like

2. Provide a simple & straightforward method for submitting referrals

3. Offer to reward them for their efforts

You can essentially enlist an army of amateur recruiters to work for the price of a Gift Card.

🏆 ACHIEVEMENTS UNLOCKED

➢ Increase Applicant Flow

➢ Increase social media engagement

➢ Reduce Sourcing Time Commitment for Recruiters & Hiring Managers

BUILD A CANDIDATE BENCH

When you receive referrals or evaluate strong candidates that don't fit a role but are still considered A-Players (perhaps in a slightly different role), add them to a "bench" of candidates that you remain engaged with periodically.

Having a strong candidate bench is the cheapest and most reliable source of A+ Talent when a new need arises. Because your network and team has already fully- or partially-evaluated the players on your bench, you have far more data on these folks than on any brand new prospect or applicant.

🏆 ACHIEVEMENTS UNLOCKED

- ➢ Maintain a relationship between Employer and A-Players
- ➢ Provide a wealth of pre-vetted candidates for new openings
- ➢ Reduce Sourcing time commitment for Recruiters & Hiring Managers
- ➢ Shorten Time-to-Hire

INCLUDE NEW HIRE TESTIMONIALS IN RECRUITMENT MARKETING

If part of an employee's first few months includes a check-in with the manager or department head, ask your new hire questions about how her experience thus far aligns with what she was sold during the Recruiting Process.

Take comprehensive notes or record the conversation, and ask her permission to use her feedback in an effort to recruit more people like her. Reference her comments in Job Postings, Culture Campaigns and other Recruitment Marketing efforts.

A New Hire's ability to add value quickly has a lot to do with her onboarding experience and the first 90-100 days of employment. Hopefully, your onboarding process includes more than a quick office tour and directions to her workstation. People love sharing their opinions and observations, and by telling your new hire you want to find more people like her, she will be flattered and 99% likely to agree to having her feedback shared publicly.

On the Marketing side, job-seekers considering a multitude of roles will see feedback from someone who is now in the situation they want to find themselves in very soon.

They'll relate more strongly to her feedback than to that of a long-tenured employee.

 ACHIEVEMENTS UNLOCKED

➢ Increase Applicant Volume
➢ Improve Employer Brand Quality

CRAFT A UNIQUE SUCCESS PROPOSITION

Whether on your own or through collaboration with your team, come up with a Unique Success Proposition of why your company is a great place to work, how working with you will make them successful and how they will make the company, its customers and its investors successful. Use this USP liberally in communication with Prospects during direct Outreach and on Job Boards.

Most job descriptions simply include a company's history, generic description as well as a bullet point list of benefits and perks. It's all very dry and corporate. Some companies do refer to their value prop as an Employer, but so few go beyond a list of benefits and perks. Crafting a Unique Success Proposition helps your company to stand out and appeal to a Job-Seeker's interests in a highly effective way.

🏆 ACHIEVEMENTS UNLOCKED

- ➢ Differentiate Employer from competing Employers
- ➢ Paint a clear picture for job seekers and prospects of how your company is better.
- ➢ Increase interest from Job-Seekers & Prospects
- ➢ Reduce Sourcing Time Commitment for Recruiters & Hiring Managers

SHARE OPPORTUNITIES IN TARGETED ONLINE COMMUNITIES

Source a list of popular online communities frequented by your Colleagues (Facebook groups, LinkedIn groups, Sub-reddits, etc.) and share information about your opening(s) and unique value proposition that is tailored to the audiences in each community.

Every company shares job openings on their first-party social media. Very few attempt to extend their social media reach much further than that. Assuming it doesn't violate community rules or standards, job openings shared by a trusted community member (your Colleague) can spark an influx of higher-quality applicants far better than the applicant traffic from a public, free job board.

🏆 ACHIEVEMENTS UNLOCKED

➢ Increase Applicant Volume
➢ Increase Applicant Quality
➢ Reduce Sourcing Time Commitment for Recruiters & Hiring Managers

PRODUCE A CULTURE VIDEO

Document day-to-day operations and special events via photo and video at a high-level. Interview colleagues, asking about their favorite aspects of working for your company. Leverage internal talent or use Fivver to produce of a brief video highlighting all the positive aspects of the company's culture. Embed or Link to the video with every Job Ad and mention of current opportunities.

99% of companies still believe they can effectively convey their value as an employer through a few sentences on a Job Ad, or that curious applicants are going to read a generic, corporate "About Us" website link. Adoption of visual media in recruitment marketing is incredibly low, and early adopters will reap the benefits of using a (literally) multi-media approach.

🏆 *ACHIEVEMENTS UNLOCKED*

- ➢ Increase Applicant Volume
- ➢ Humanize the Employer & Team
- ➢ Improve Employer Brand quality
- ➢ Improve Internal Morale

PUBLISH EMPLOYEE PROFILES

Once per month, or every few weeks, pretend you're a biographer researching a colleague. Ask him about his employment history, what it's like been different about working at your company compared to previous jobs he's held. Ask a handful of his peers what it's like working with him. Publish the profile with transcripts, photos, video clips etc.

Not only does this provide a human face for your Company (many faces, actually), the message it conveys to Prospects and Job-Seekers is "We care about our people". This type of highly-personalized content also comes with an added benefit: Employees, their coworkers, their friends, their family will all share & reshare this content on social media, resulting in a mini-viral effect that provides free exposure to potential applicants.

🏆 **ACHIEVEMENTS UNLOCKED**

➤ Increase Applicant Volume
➤ Humanize the Employer and Team
➤ Improve Employer Brand quality
➤ Improve Internal Morale

LAUNCH A CULTURE CAMPAIGN

Similar to the previous two strategies, but more organized & intentional. Work with your marketing team (or an outside consultancy) to develop a content marketing strategy completely focused on internal operations and company culture. Publish this content on a regular schedule to social media to maximize breadth & depth of exposure.

As Gary Vaynerchuk (@garyvee) puts it, "every company is a media company" in the Internet Age. While that means successful companies need to provide useful & entertaining content to their customers, the same is true for your recruiting efforts. In recruiting, your customers are A-Player candidates and your "leads" are the prospects that aren't yet fully aware of your company & job opportunities. According to a Glassdoor Report[7], "Organizations that invest in employer branding are three times more likely to make a quality hire."

Launching a culture campaign naturally increases interest & engagement in your employment opportunities, now and in the future.

🏆 ACHIEVEMENTS UNLOCKED

- ➢ Improve Employer Brand Quality
- ➢ Increase Applicant Volume
- ➢ Convert curious Job-Seekers into Engaged Applicants
- ➢ Improve Overall Company/Brand awareness
- ➢ Improve Internal Morale

HIGHLIGHT LOCATION & SCHEDULING BENEFITS

Is your office location easily accessible? Do you provide free parking? Is "flexible scheduling" a core cultural belief? Conveying the importance of convenient work-life balance factors can make a world of difference at every stage, from sourcing through evaluation.

Location, Location, Location. Work/Life Balance. These are cliches, but they exist for good reason. Work/Life balance, schedule flexibility & other convenience factors are increasingly becoming an important factor in decisions made by Job-Seekers. In fact, *HIRED* reports that 40% of candidates cite Location & Commute as a reason for leaving a company for a new opportunity[8]. While no location is 100% perfect, offerings like partial remote work and flexible scheduling can be used strategically as a competitive advantage to entice prospects into the recruiting process.

🏆 *ACHIEVEMENTS UNLOCKED*

- ➤ Increase Prospect Engagement
- ➤ Convert Curious Prospects Into Engaged Candidates
- ➤ Increase Inbound Applicant Flow
- ➤ Improve Internal Morale

SPONSOR INDUSTRY EVENTS

Set aside time & budget to have your company included as a sponsor for Meetups, Conferences & other events that draw interest from potential A-Players. Request an opportunity for you or a peer to briefly pitch your Company and current openings at the event.

A-Players are eternal students. They love their craft, and they're constantly seeking out ways to improve & new learning opportunities. If you do the proper research, you can find the events most likely to attract A-Players in a particular set of disciplines, giving you a concentrated talent pool & captive audience to whom you can present your Company & opportunities.

🏆 ACHIEVEMENTS UNLOCKED

➢ Improve Employer Brand Quality
➢ Increase Applicant Volume
➢ Improve Overall Company/Brand Awareness

ENCOURAGE PRESENTATION & SPEAKING OPPORTUNITIES WITH TEAM MEMBERS & COMPANY LEADERSHIP

Encourage internal Lunch-and-Learn topics and sharing of ideas, that can then be improved incrementally and pitched as Meetup & Event speaking topics by your individual contributors & leadership. Share accounts of these presentations on Social Media.

High-caliber, highly desirable teams encourage the sharing of innovation and new ideas in general. A-Players want to go where teams and individuals welcome open debate of ideas and suggestions. The knowledge that your organization is willing to debate and experiment with creative ideas will increase the likelihood that they'll engage with your opportunities.

🏆 ACHIEVEMENTS UNLOCKED

➢ Improve Employer Brand Quality
➢ Increase Applicant Volume
➢ Improve internal morale

ENLIST AN EXPERT COPYWRITER TO REWRITE YOUR JOB AD

Consult with a copywriting expert to reorganize and rewrite your position description to deliver a balance of critical information with persuasive language.

When you post a position to a Job Board, your primary objective is to stand out amongst the hundreds of similar Ads from competing Employers, converting window-shopping job-seekers into interested applicants. 99.9% of Hiring Managers composing job ads are not seasoned copywriters, thus they are leaving potential conversions on the table. For a minimal investment, someone with a persuasive copywriting skill-set can identify and fix the areas of your Job Ad that are not appealing to your target audience.

🏆 ACHIEVEMENTS UNLOCKED

- ➤ Increase Inbound Applicant Flow
- ➤ Improve Employer Brand Quality

CODIFY & PUBLISH COMPANY VALUES

Beginning with your Leadership Team, followed by input from your employees, determine the most important values that team members strive to personify in their day-to-day work. Select the most common and most important values, codify it, and publish these values everywhere. Provide examples of how team members have exhibited these values. Publish your values on your website, on your Job Ads, in communication with Prospects and Candidates. Everywhere.

Most Employers don't have a clearly-articulated culture or defined set of values. Most of those that do simply pay lip service to their values, rather than actually bothering to embody them. Even companies who live their values & culture fail to share who they are and how they work together until a candidate is already entrenched in the Evaluation process.

Failing to share your culture and values with job-seekers is a huge wasted opportunity. A-Players want to understand not just what you do but who you are. Publishing legitimate values is likely the one thing guaranteed not only to differentiate your organization from all your Employer competition, but also to attract the right type of A-Player

Applicants while deterring those who aren't interested in (or capable of) embodying those values.

 ACHIEVEMENTS UNLOCKED

➢ Increase Applicant Volume
➢ Improve Employer Brand Quality

ACKNOWLEDGE EMPLOYER REPUTATION SHORTCOMINGS

No Employer has a perfect reputation. Identify weaknesses & shortcomings by soliciting feedback from current and outgoing team members, as well as from review sites like Glassdoor. In conversations with prospects and candidates, openly acknowledge that you're far from perfect, and that you are constantly striving to make your environment a great place to work.

Technology, in particular Social Media and "Web 2.0" style platforms, has created an environment where reputation is front-and-center, and it is perhaps the most important thing for any company to actively manage. According to HIRED, 46% of job-seekers will not consider applying for an opportunity if the company has a poor reputation.

A poor reputation can't be ignored or brushed under the carpet, nor can a company fix the perception by refuting the damning claims. The only truly effective path to improve a damaged reputation is through increased transparency.

By acknowledging legitimate issues and working towards improvement, the company is saying, "We know we have some issues, and we want to be better." There is perhaps nothing more relatable to an A-Player than imperfection combined with humility and a desire for continuous improvement.

ACHIEVEMENTS UNLOCKED

- ➤ Increase Employer-Candidate Trust
- ➤ Improve Employer Brand Quality

PROFILE YOUR LEADERSHIP TEAM

Put on your biographer hat and interview your company's leadership. Ask them about their previous experiences, their journey to their current status, and how this role differs from their previous leadership positions. Inquire about what leadership means to them. Talk to their direct reports about what it's like having this person as a manager and leader. Publish the profile with transcripts, photos, video clips etc.

A popular saying suggests that, "People don't leave jobs, they leave managers." Logic and reason would suggest, then, that people don't just join a company because of the compensation & benefits. They join because they believe in the management and leadership that is guiding your Company to realize its vision. Humanizing your leadership team is a relatively low-cost effort that can reap great rewards in the form of high volume A-Player applications.

🏆 ACHIEVEMENTS UNLOCKED

- ➤ Improve Employer Brand Quality
- ➤ Increase Applicant Volume
- ➤ Humanize the Employer & Team
- ➤ Improve Internal Morale

OUTLINE PROBLEMS THEY GET TO SOLVE

In Job Ads and while engaging with promising Prospects, go into detail about the challenges the organization is facing, the gains you hope to make and the accomplishments towards which this role will contribute.

An A-Player is primarily motivated by solving problems, getting $#@~ done, and achieving outcomes. By putting focus on how her contribution will lead to the achievement of team & company goals, you'll naturally appeal to her desire for success and accomplishment.

Most companies choose to highlight activities and outputs in their position descriptions and job ads, and while a basic understanding of activities & responsibilities is important, A-Players aren't interested in what they're going to be told to do. They 100% prefer knowing what needs to get done and why it's important.

🏆 **ACHIEVEMENTS UNLOCKED**

➤ Improve Prospect Engagement Rate
➤ Increase Applicant Volume
➤ Improve Employer Brand Quality

SOLVE THEIR PROBLEMS

Identify the pain points of your A-Player candidate. Does she want more autonomy? More growth or better growth opportunities?

Does your Opportunity, Company Vision, & Company Culture potentially solve any of these problems? If so, call attention to the problems and explain how your job is the solution she's been seeking.

Engaging Prospects & Candidates is a Sales Process, plain and simple. In Sales, there are two primary approaches that convert leads into prospects & prospects into customers. The first is to solve one or more painful problems for the target. The second is to sell your lead an "aspirational identity", painting a picture of who they could become by taking advantage of your opportunity.

In many situations, the people you engage with are seeking to escape specific pains of their current employment situation. If you can learn to identify & empathize with these pains, AND if your opportunity can relieve the pain, you can appeal to this desire in any candidate and motivate them to engage fully in your recruiting process.

🏆 ACHIEVEMENTS UNLOCKED

- ➤ Increase Prospect Engagement Rates
- ➤ Convert Curious Prospects Into Engaged Candidates
- ➤ Increase Applicant Volume

SELL AN ASPIRATIONAL IDENTITY

Through discussion and discovery, determine what the immediate and long-term potential opportunities are for an A-Player in your open role. In Prospect or Candidate discussions, sell them on who they could potentially become if they commit to the evaluation process.

Engaging Outbound Leads is a Sales Process. In Sales, there are two primary approaches that convert leads into prospects & prospects into customers. The first is to solve one or more painful problems for the target. The second is to sell your lead an "aspirational identity", painting a picture of who they could become by taking advantage of your opportunity.

The biggest unspoken question on the mind of any candidate is, "Who do I get to be if I come to work with you?" If you're an early-stage startup offering a fast-paced environment & a fast-track of advancement, that will appeal to a certain type of A-Player. If your stable, steady growth allows her to be a contributor with a dependable schedule, tell her. If she gets the chance to mentor, grow & shape a team in her image, that will appeal to a slightly different type of A-Player. The key is to ensure that your needs align with your candidate's strengths and desires.

ACHIEVEMENTS UNLOCKED

➢ Increase Prospect Engagement Rates

➢ Convert Curious Prospects Into Engaged Candidates

➢ Increase Applicant Volume

SOURCE 24/7/365

Always be sourcing potential candidates for the types of roles you may be hiring in the future, regardless of whether you're actively seeking to fill one of those positions.

Do you typically identify a hiring need months before you need to fill the role? Unlikely. Most of the time you needed that person hired, onboarded, and adding value to your organization ... well, yesterday. Just the process of defining a role, composing a Job Ad and announcing it to the world can take weeks, which means you're even more behind schedule.

If you're constantly taking note of really talented people across a variety of skills and disciplines, you can actually be proactive and get out in front of filling an open position rather than starting from scratch with every new opening.

Also, employee turnover is a painful reality for everyone. Regardless of what your turnover rates are, people will inevitably leave for other opportunities, and you will have to backfill them. Sourcing only when actively hiring is short-sighted and only makes it take a lot longer to fill a position after it's been opened.

ACHIEVEMENTS UNLOCKED

> ➤ Supplement Candidate Bench

> ➤ Shorten Time-to-Hire

PART THREE

SCREENING

Once your role and/or company reach a certain notoriety, your primary sourcing challenge is no longer a problem of too few candidates.

Now it's an issue of too many candidates, most of whom don't meet B- or even C-Player status.

You need a preliminary screening mechanism to start finding the signal amongst all the noise, and do so quickly before the qualified Candidates lose interest.

This screening mechanism will qualify applicants on basic competence and general interest.

Implement one or more of the Screening Mechanisms to effectively AND efficiently advance the Qualified Candidate to the Evaluation Stage.

TRAIN OTHERS TO REVIEW APPLICATIONS

Invite managers and emerging leaders to observe and ask questions as you filter out unqualified Applicants and advance others to the Screening or Evaluation stage. Take notes and internally document standards, Applicant red flags, etc. for future reference.

For any position that receives a high volume of applications, the #1 biggest choke point is in reviewing Applicants and culling qualified applicants from a massive pile of résumés.

This is also the most critical point in the Recruiting Process where Employers cannot afford inefficiency.

A+ Talent is going to be applying to multiple companies, and a first-mover advantage can make or break your chances of hiring that A-Player before your competition does.

By training and entrusting others on what you look for in an Applicant, you free yourself from inevitably becoming a single point of failure in the Recruiting machine.

🏆 **ACHIEVEMENTS UNLOCKED**

➤ Shorten Overall Cycle Time
➤ Improve Candidate Experience
➤ Improve Employee Engagement

ADD SCREENING QUESTIONS TO YOUR APPLICATION

Add 4-5 Screening Questions as a pre-condition for Applications to be submitted.

Technology has shifted balance of power to the Job-Seeker, at least as it pertains to applying for open opportunities. Interested Job-Seekers barely need to do more than click a few links or send an attachment via to apply nowadays, which means they can apply in high volume to positions they may not even have much interest in. Including a handful of short-answer questions that doubles as your Screening mechanism introduces just enough barrier to entry to filter out those Job-Seekers who only serve as clutter at the top of your Candidate Funnel.

🏆 ACHIEVEMENTS UNLOCKED

➢ Shorten Screening Cycle Time
➢ Filter Out Low-Interest Job-Seekers

LEVERAGE A 3RD PARTY ASSESSMENT TOOL

Subscribe to an online Testing & Assessment Platform which offers a variety of templated assessments that can be easily shared with and completed by Applicants. Many of these platforms offer free trials and affordable entry-level pricing tiers.

The need for easier Screening automation has produced a wide assortment of assessment & testing tools across a variety of disciplines. Platforms like Hacker Rank offer turnkey and customized testing solutions for technical positions like Software Developers & Quality Assurance Engineers, as well as non-technical quizzes & questionnaires.

🏆 **ACHIEVEMENTS UNLOCKED**

➤ Filter Out Low-Interest Applicants
➤ Reduce Sourcing Time Commitments for Recruiters & Hiring Managers

---

HIRE A 3RD PARTY SCREENING SERVICE

Hire a B2B Service that handles scheduling, performing, recording, and potentially grading the Screening phase, based on a format and questions of your choosing.

The Screening phase should always be as uniform as possible for all Applicants. Due to the uniform and repeatable nature of this phase, it can often be outsourced to a 3rd party service. While these solutions may come with a considerable price-tag, Recruiters and Hiring Managers should consider the value of their time-savings when analyzing the cost-benefit proposition of a 3rd party service.

🏆 ACHIEVEMENTS UNLOCKED

➢ Reduce Screening Time Commitment for Recruiters & Hiring Managers

SOURCE SCREENING RECOMMENDATIONS FROM COLLEAGUES

Survey your current staff, asking them what types of Screening procedures they've participated in during past recruiting experiences. Find out what their favorites have been and why.

You have a wealth of historical Candidate Experiences right under your nose: Your existing team of A-Players. There's absolutely no need to reinvent the wheel when it comes to Screening mechanisms. By finding out which experiences they found the most interesting and engaging, you're sure to find ideas guaranteed to be interesting and engaging to the A-Players in your current group of Applicants, that you can then adapt and apply to your own process.

🏆 ACHIEVEMENTS UNLOCKED

➤ Increase Employee Engagement

➤ Improve Candidate Experience

KEEP SCREENS BRIEF

An initial screen should take no longer than 30 minutes to complete. In most cases, this means limiting a screening system to no more than 4-5 short answer questions or a brief skill-based exercise.

The screening stage is not intended to be a comprehensive evaluation process. If you set up too many hurdles for applicants, you will experience a diminished % of high-quality applicants completing the screen, and potentially you will find detailed accounts of your demanding screening process plastered all over sites like Glassdoor.

A+ Talent is in high demand and will likely be considering multiple opportunities, so your screening mechanism should only serve to provide clarity to you, the Employer, on answers to a few questions:

1. Has the applicant demonstrated she is competent in the discipline of this role?
2. Can the applicant articulate clear examples of previous experiences in a related role or capacity?
3. Does the quality of effort made by the applicant during screening suggest she would be interested in continuing to the Evaluation stage?

🏆 ACHIEVEMENTS UNLOCKED

- ➤ Increase Screening Completion Rates
- ➤ Improve Screening Response Quality
- ➤ Filter Out Low-Interest Applicants
- ➤ Reduce Screening Time Commitment for Recruiters & Mgrs

IMPLEMENT AN ANSWERING SERVICE

Sign up with a phone answering service like *CallHippo* or *AccessDirect* that allows callers to leave answers of unrestricted length. In your job description or application process, include a short list of screening questions and instruct applicants to call the number and record a message with their answers to each question.

Anyone who has tried both written and phone screening methods will attest that a phone screen is the superior approach, producing higher quality & more reliable initial assessments. That said, time constraints can limit a busy Manager's ability to perform a manual phone screen when facing a high volume of applications.

The answering service allows for automating the process while still receiving valuable context found in the inflection, tone, & other aspects of an applicants orated responses. Also, it requires an applicant to put forth just enough effort to indicate she's truly interested in your opportunity.

🏆 ACHIEVEMENTS UNLOCKED

➢ Improve Screening Response Quality
➢ Filter Out Low-Interest Applicants
➢ Reduce Screening Time Commitment for Recruiters & Hiring Managers

LEVERAGE A CHEAP/FREE ONLINE FORM QUESTIONNAIRE

Create a short form-based screening tool using an affordable tool like Google Forms or Typeform. When a job-seeker applies for your role, automatically e-mail them , a short description on the purpose of the screen, and a link to complete the form.

If money is tight, leveraging a low- or no-cost custom online form provides a single place for Applicants to complete your Screening requirement. While this is an additional step to the application process, not all application sources will support adding your screening questions to the application process.

To ensure a strong completion rate, it is critical to try and automate sending this e-mail, so that Applicants can complete the Screening step while your opportunity is still top of mind. Delay delivery by even 30 minutes, and your Applicant has had her attention stolen by a dozen other things.

🏆 **ACHIEVEMENTS UNLOCKED**

➢ Increase Screening Completion Rate
➢ Reduce Screening Time Commitment for Recruiters & Hiring Managers

---

SEND AN E-MAIL QUESTIONNAIRE

When a job-seeker applies for your role, automatically e-mail them , a short description on the purpose of the screen, and a list of questions to answer in an e-mail reply.

This is the lowest-cost, lowest-fidelity Screening solution. Much like the Online Form strategy, this does add one more step to the application process, which is often not preferable but could be if you receive a high volume of unqualified Applicants. Also, some Applicant sources won't support custom questions in the application process.

I can't stress enough that you must try to automate sending this e-mail to be synchronous with receive an Application, so that Applicants can complete the Screening step while your opportunity is still top of mind. A-Players will grow weary of your process if they continually have to set aside and schedule time to jump through another (albeit important) hoop.

🏆 **ACHIEVEMENTS UNLOCKED**

➢ Increase Screening Completion Rate
➢ Reduce Screening Time Commitment For Recruiters & Hiring Managers

---

PART FOUR
EVALUATING

Along with unclear role expectations & poor candidate sourcing, the 3rd biggest contributor to poor hiring decisions is a lack of confidence in your ability to evaluate candidates & make a hiring decision.

Evaluation cannot be effective if it is contentious, unfocused, repetitive, or disjointed.

Use these Strategies to improve the Accuracy of your Interviews as well as the Enjoyment of the Evaluation Stage for all parties involved.

STAFF YOUR INTERVIEWS WITH PEOPLE SIMILAR TO YOUR CANDIDATE

When conducting in-person evaluations, make every attempt to involve at least one Interviewer who is similar to the candidate in one or more tangible ways. Some examples include:

- Cultural similarities
- Appearance
- Age range
- Gender
- Previous Employers
- Shared alma mater
- Shared interests

Interviews are often an awkward dance in the courtship process between the Candidate and you as a potential Employer. Both sides are often so focused on conveying their best selves that truths become embellished, or embellishments turn into outright lies. So how can you ensure that the answers a Candidate provides are a reflection of reality?

One simple way is to get them feeling comfortable right from the outset. A person is far more likely to stretch the truth when they feel defensive, anxious or stressed. Someone who feels comfortable will more readily admit to mistakes made, lessons learned, and blind spots.

The Rule of Liking states that people are far more likely to follow the influence of those they know and like. By demonstrating shared traits or experiences with someone in the room, you'll get them to feel safe and open up much more effectively.

🏆 ACHIEVEMENTS UNLOCKED

➢ Quickly & Easily Establish a Comfortable Environment

➢ Increase Employer-Candidate Trust Levels

➢ Improve Candidness & Honesty

➢ Improve Candidate Experience

RETIRE BRAINTEASERS & "CLEVER" QUESTIONS

For evaluating general cognitive ability, intangible strengths and culture fit, replace Brainteasers and so-called "clever" examinations with clear, experience-focused questions.

Tech giants like Google were once famed for asking Candidates brain-teasers in an attempt to gauge cognitive ability & problem-solving skills.

Yet, in his New York Times Bestseller *Work Rules*, Google's former SVP of People Operations, Laszlo Bock, specifically denounces these types of puzzles as ineffective, writing, "we learned that doing well in solo competitions doesn't always translate into being a team player […] Or they are accustomed to solving problems with finite ends and clear solutions, rather than navigating the complexity of real-world challenges."[9]

At the same time, thousands of Interviewers and Hiring Managers have one or two "pet questions" that they believe will tell them everything they need to know about a Candidate ("If you could be any animal …" ring a bell?). If I'm your Candidate, and I told you I would be a cheetah, and your answer is also "cheetah", all that tells you is we're both familiar with fast, exotic felines native to Africa.

🏆 *ACHIEVEMENTS UNLOCKED*

➢ Improve Evaluation Accuracy
➢ Improve Candidate Experience

BUILD AN INTERVIEWER BULLPEN

Enlist members of your team with diverse disciplines, levels of experience, and backgrounds to lead and participate in the Interview process. Provide formal training on your Interviewing methods, and continually introduce fresh blood into the process via shadowing techniques.

Perhaps the most common mistake made by Hiring Managers is involving themselves in every step of the Screening & Evaluation stages. While there certainly can be advantages found in this amount of consistency, every Manager is also juggling dozens of other responsibilities in addition to Candidate Evaluation. Having a trusted bullpen of great Interviewers you can call on at a moment's notice allows you to more easily optimize and scale your Recruiting efforts as you continue to grow. It also eliminates the risk of alienating and losing Candidates due to Interview delays, rescheduling or canceling because a single person became unavailable.

🏆 ACHIEVEMENTS UNLOCKED

➤ Reduce Time Commitment to Evaluation by Hiring Manager

➤ Improve Evaluation Effectiveness

➤ Shorten Evaluation Cycle Time

COMPILE & PUBLISH AN INTERNAL QUESTION BANK

Build, Buy and Borrow a list of trusted Interview questions, and publish the list somewhere that's easily accessible in your internal company network. For bonus points, describe the intent of the question and what Interviewers should hope to learn from a Candidate's answers.

A big challenge arises when Evaluating multiple qualified Candidates for a single role. Not only are their skills & experiences never the same, but often the questions asked by Interviewers are wildly different, which means that different Candidates were not Evaluated for the same strengths & weaknesses. This can lead to Interviewer feedback being very "gut-based", which is simply a nice way of saying "biased".

It's not that every Interview should follow the same exact script of identical questions, but it should be clear to Interviewers what you need to evaluate and what types of questions are best suited to meet that need.

🏆 **ACHIEVEMENTS UNLOCKED**

➢ Shorten Interviewer Onboarding
➢ Improve Evaluation Consistency
➢ Improve Evaluation Accuracy

PRESS CANDIDATES FOR DETAIL WITH FOLLOW-UP QUESTIONS

Follow nearly every primary question in an Interview with at least one follow-up question. The follow-up can be as simple as "Could you provide some specifics?", "Why do you think it happened that way?", or "What would you have done differently?"

In any Interview scenario, the Employer holds a distinct advantage: The Interviewers know the questions ahead of time, and the Candidate doesn't. For many personality types, when presented with a question they don't immediately have an answer to, they will freeze up and provide an incomplete answer, or a complete non-answer. "I'm not sure." "Not really." "Maybe once or twice."

Asking a follow-up question with sincere curiosity gives the Candidate the time and ability to jog her memory and access more information.

Think about the last conversation you had with a person you'd just met. Did you dive deeply into any particular topic, or did it feel like you just skimmed the surface? Avoiding the desire to skip to the next topic, and instead asking a series of curious follow-ups, will help both the

Candidate and the Interviewers to paint a clearer and more realistic picture of the Candidate's abilities & experiences.

🏆 ACHIEVEMENTS UNLOCKED

➤ Improve Candidate's Engagement in Interviews

➤ Improve Evaluation Accuracy

STANDARDIZE FEEDBACK FROM INTERVIEWERS

Build a universal format and delivery mechanism to collect, review and discuss Interviewer feedback within 24 hours of completing an interview (ideally same-day). Provide explicit definitions and explanations for any skill or strength area that may potentially be unclear to or misinterpreted by Interviewers. Formats will differ between positions based on technical skills & competencies and will typically share in grading common intangible strengths such as communication skills & humility.

Far too many Evaluation systems are disorganized, unstructured and chaotic. That is to say, they aren't systems at all. And while members of the Interview team should and probably do have a decent sense of what the open role, it's usually only the Hiring Manager who has a 100% clear mental image of who their A-Player is. Thus, it's the Hiring Manager who needs to gather and discuss as much objective, unbiased feedback as possible to make a decision on a particular Candidate.

Providing Interviewers with a list of questions they must be able to answer about the candidate, or a series of qualities & skills on which they'll have to grade the Candidate, serves a number of useful purposes.

Question Bank Benefits:

- It sets expectations -- both for the Candidate's capabilities and the Interviewer's performance
- It better prepares all Interviewers before each Interview
- It provides them with a handy note-taking resource during Interviews
- It eliminates worry of Interviewers not providing thorough & valuable feedback.

 ACHIEVEMENTS UNLOCKED

➢ Reduce Bias in Evaluations

➢ Improve Feedback Quality

➢ Improve Evaluation Accuracy

QUESTIONS FOR CULTURE, EXERCISES FOR SKILLSET

Divide your in-depth Interviews into a minimum of two parts:
1. A period allotted for inquiring about their prior experiences in communication, collaboration, leadership, conflict resolution, etc.
2. Dedicated time to lead the candidate through a discipline-specific exercise that simulates one or more real-world activities they would be performing on the job.

All too often, Employers spend an entire Interview session asking candidates technical / skill-set questions to determine if they can talk about performing in a role similar to the role you're evaluating them for. The problem with this approach is that crafty candidates can BS their way through Q&A, using technical jargon and industry buzzwords to give the impression that they're competent. Failing to evaluate a candidate's actual ability to perform in the role -- not just her ability to say she can -- often leads to hiring mistakes, wasting tens or hundreds of thousands of dollars compensating an incapable new hire.

There is no more reliable way to evaluate a candidate's technical strengths -- whether that strength is coding, multi-tasking, or conflict resolution, than to simulate a situation or challenge that they could face on the job in your position. Combining these types of exercises with a standard, structured set of questions about her past experiences will allow you to construct a more complete picture of her cognitive abilities, intangible strengths and discipline-specific competencies.

ACHIEVEMENTS UNLOCKED

➤ Improve Assessment Effectiveness
➤ Improve Candidate Experience

MAKE EXERCISES INTERACTIVE

For all simulated exercises, ensure the Interview is populated with people from your team who are able to evaluate the appropriate competencies in your candidate, and that they're familiar with the goals & execution of the Exercise. Implore the candidate to ask questions of Interviewers and solicit input and feedback during the exercise. DON'T Provide the candidate a list of and leave her to complete a solo exercise.

99% of Information Workers operate in a team environment every single day. Thus, the Evaluation stage must include ways to gauge a Candidate's ability to work with 1 or more people in an effort to produce a defined output.

Studies indicate that a person's ability to solve a problem in isolation is ineffective at predicting her ability to perform in a team environment.

By simulating a collaborative situation using existing team members, you can more accurately assess a candidate's ability to make suggestions, ask questions and manage feedback in your unique environment.

🏆 ACHIEVEMENTS UNLOCKED

- ➤ Evaluate Collaboration Abilities
- ➤ Improve Candidate Experience

COMPILE AN EXERCISE BANK

Collaborate with your team to develop a handful of standard Skill Evaluation Exercises to assess particular critical skills & strengths. Train members of your Interviewer Bullpen on leading candidates through each Exercise. Rely solely on the established bank of standard exercises, Gradually improving them over time. Retire an Exercise only when it no longer serves to effectively assess those skills -OR- when it's been so widely published that Candidates are consistently able to "cheat" their way through it.

An effective Skill Evaluation Exercise clearly outlines the expected output or result but allows for a variety of paths to success. Because there is no single "answer" to produce the output, these exercises can (and should) be re-used, iterated upon, and improved over time. By using the same exercise in evaluating multiple candidates, you reduce the number of variable elements and are better equipped to grade & compare the relative performance of each candidate.

NOTE: These exercises can become stale over a longer period of time, so it's important to assess their effectiveness a couple times each year.

🏆 ACHIEVEMENTS UNLOCKED

➤ Improve Evaluation Consistency

➤ Improve Evaluation Accuracy

➤ Prevents "Clever Interviewer" Syndrome

EVALUATE FOR EMERGENT LEADERSHIP

Ask a Candidate direct questions that draw from her experience demonstrating perseverance, trustworthiness, fairness, etc. Inquire about specific examples, ask follow-up questions to go deeper into her stories, and confirm these specific accounts during Reference Checks. A Candidate's answers to this line of questioning will tell you whether she has the capacity to lead regardless of role or title.

In a Forbes article "8 Ways to Assess Leadership", contributor Margaret M. Perlis outlines what she refers to as the Eight Pillars of Character. They are

1. Fortitude
2. Temperance/Responsibility
3. Prudence
4. Justice/Fairness
5. Trustworthiness
6. Respect
7. Caring
8. Citizenship

Regardless of whether you're hiring a People Manager or explicit Leadership role, any skilled, intelligent Candidate who also embodies these traits will be capable of knowing when to lead an initiative, when to follow another's lead, and is in general far more likely to be an A+ Team Player.

🏆 ACHIEVEMENTS UNLOCKED

- ➢ Improve Evaluation Accuracy
- ➢ Improve Culture Fit Evaluation

EVALUATE FOR EXPERIENCES OVERCOMING ADVERSITY

In Screening and Evaluation Stages, ask a Candidate to describe experiences in her life and work where she had to overcome adversity. Ask follow-up questions about how she felt throughout the process, who she sought out for help, how she felt afterwards, and what she would do differently.

During a Skill Evaluation Exercise, tweak one or two conditions slightly that would force a candidate to adapt and potentially change her approach.

Interviews can (and should) be both highly educational for Interviewers as well as enjoyable for Candidates. So what better way to learn about a Candidate than to ask her to talk about her favorite topic: Herself! A-Players are not only incredibly proud of the obstacles they've overcome in their career and life, but they welcome new challenges. They thrive on the satisfaction of achieving some outcome, simulated or otherwise.

🏆 ACHIEVEMENTS UNLOCKED

➤ Improve Evaluation Accuracy
➤ Improve Candidate Experience

SHARE THE AGENDA AT INTERVIEW OUTSET

As you initiate the Interview with your Candidate, give a brief overview of the different segments that will make up the Interview. Tell her you'll be inquiring about past experiences, challenges, strengths, etc. Inform her whether there will be any hands-on exercises and at what point those would take place. Let her know if and when she'll be given time to ask questions.

The goal of a lengthy Interview should be solely to Evaluate a Candidate's ability to overcome the obstacles and produce the type of outputs that would achieve desired outcomes that make the person in this role successful. You absolutely should be learning about the Candidate and testing her experiences and strengths.

You shouldn't aim to trick, surprise, or make a Candidate feel inferior & uncomfortable. By showing just enough of your hand at the outset, sharing the high-level agenda, a Candidate has one less unknown to worry about, putting her slightly more at-ease and able to focus solely on answering your questions and participating in the exercises.

ACHIEVEMENTS UNLOCKED

➤ Improve Candidate Experience

➤ Quickly & Easily Establish a Comfortable Environment

➤ Increase Employer-Candidate Trust Levels

➤ Improve Candidness & Honesty

PART FIVE

CLOSING

Next to an inability to source quality candidates, the most frustrating experience for any Hiring Manager is losing highly desirable candidates due to being unable to close on offer acceptance.

Making an enticing offer goes beyond simple salary and benefits. It is its own mini-sales process.

No two candidates are exactly alike, thus no offer package will universally appeal to 100% of A-Player Candidates.

In order to close a high % of candidates, you must be tuned into what motivates a candidate.

Experiment with these Strategies to see a higher % of your Offers accepted in record time.

MAKE YOURSELF (AND YOUR TEAM) EASILY ACCESSIBLE

After sending the formal Offer and discussing it with the Candidate, give her your contact information as well as an easy way to contact others she's met so she can discuss any concerns and ask any questions she may have. This can be as formal as providing e-mail addresses or as personal as providing a cellphone number.

Whether we admit it or not, a Candidate's decision on whether to accept a new opportunity is a highly individual and personal decision. That means that, even with the support of family and friends, it can be a very isolating and lonely decision-making process.

When you're making a life-changing decision AND you feel alone, the best feeling comes from the knowledge you're actually not 100% alone and help is just a call, text or email away.

By putting in just a little extra effort and providing her with a handful of people she can connect with, it makes the process feel far less lonely, even if she never takes you up on the offer to reach out.

ACHIEVEMENTS UNLOCKED

- ➢ Improve Candidate Experience
- ➢ Improve Employer Brand Quality
- ➢ Increase Offer Acceptance Rate

OVER-DELIVER ON DETAIL

Both in distributing and discussing an Offer with a Candidate, provide her with any possible detail that makes her decision less uncertain. Leave no stone unturned in describing benefits, perks, values & culture. Reiterate growth opportunities provided by the opportunity and the company at large. Tell her what her onboarding experience *will* be like, who she *will* be meeting, training, & working with.

People are both rational & emotional beings. We make a high percentage of our decisions for emotional reasons, and then justify those same decisions to ourselves and others with logic. Nobody buys a Tesla because of the gas savings and low maintenance costs. They buy a Tesla because they can see themselves sitting in the driver's seat, and they love how it makes them feel. Then they tell family & friends how much money they'll save on fuel & upkeep to justify the decision.

So, provide your Candidate with both the story, the emotional image, of who she can become in short-order as well as the logical, rational foundation she can use to justify the decision.

🏆 ACHIEVEMENTS UNLOCKED

- ➢ Increase Offer Acceptance Rate
- ➢ Improve Employer Brand Quality
- ➢ Shorten Closing Stage Cycle Time

SEND THE OFFER AND CALL TO REVIEW

Instead of simply sending a detailed Offer Letter, connect with the candidate via phone or video chat. If they're unavailable when you call, find a time she's available ASAP. Tell her you'd like to review the details of the Offer and answer any questions she or her family may have.

For a moment, put yourself in the shoes of your chosen Candidate. While you are looking to add another talented member to your growing team, she is deciding on the one company to whom she will be committing half her waking hours for the next few years. Her commute is changing, her schedule, her familiar routine. Her life and the lives of those close to her will be impacted by this decision. She's replacing a lot of knowns with a world of uncertainty: New company, new manager, new teammates, new expectations. She may be having some doubts about her ability to succeed. For her, this decision is extremely personal. This is not the time to fire-and-forget a templated e-mail for the sake of efficiency.

By connecting with your candidate via phone or video chat and walking her through each piece of the Offer, she feels like more than a number. Every minute you spend answering questions, providing clarity, and allaying her fears, she will feel more valued and more confident in her decision to take this leap into the unknown.

🏆 ACHIEVEMENTS UNLOCKED

- ➢ Increase Offer Acceptance Rate
- ➢ Improve Candidate Engagement
- ➢ Shorten Time to Close

SET A REASONABLE OFFER EXPIRATION

If you find a candidate hesitating, wavering or behaving in a non-committal way, let her know that you understand the weight of her decision, and that because of the importance of filling this role, you'll need a decision by [Date] before moving on to another candidate. The date you select will vary based on the health of your Candidate pipeline, seniority of the position, and other important factors.

Think back to the last time you were on the fence about a significant purchase or life decision. You knew you wanted to pull the trigger, but you kept hesitating. Then, suddenly, you discovered that the sale price would expire in 3 days, or there was only 1 SUV with your favorite options left on the lot.

When we have an impression that our decision-making window is wide open, we will put off making a decision because there is no consequence to indecision. When we're then compelled into making a decision by an agent of urgency or scarcity, everything becomes more real as we consider only our realistic options.

🏆 *ACHIEVEMENTS UNLOCKED*

- ➤ Introduce Urgency
- ➤ Introduce Scarcity
- ➤ Shorten Closing Cycle Time

BE TRANSPARENT ABOUT OTHER CANDIDATES

When discussing an offer with a Candidate, be explicit about the number of other promising Candidates who are engaged in the various stages of your Recruiting Process. If you have other Candidates you've Evaluated and would consider for the role, tell her. If you have 5 other promising Candidates scheduled for Interviews over the next week, let her know you'll be Evaluating 5 promising Candidates in the next week.

Vague, cliché statements like "We're still considering other applicants" are typically received as little more than a nudge or thinly-veiled warnings. They're usually viewed as petty and a little contentious.

However, getting just a little specific by including numbers and timelines makes things very real, introduces a sense of urgency in the Candidate's decision-making process and just a hint of FOMO (Fear of Missing Out) that can persuade them to be decisive.

🏆 *ACHIEVEMENTS UNLOCKED*

- ➢ Introduce Urgency
- ➢ Increase Transparency & Trust
- ➢ Shorten Closing Stage Cycle Time

FEED HER INTERESTS, SOLVE HER CHALLENGES, AND ALLAY HER FEARS

Highlight each and every area where your opportunity aligns with what you've learned while discussing your unique, once-in-a-lifetime opportunity with your chosen candidate. Call attention to:

- How your opportunity presents new, unique challenges
- How she'll develop and grow in her career
- Specific glowing, positive feedback the Interview team gave after meeting her
- The problems she's experiencing that will be solved when she joins your team
- How employment with your organization makes her worries & fears unnecessary or irrelevant

Put yourself in the Candidate's shoes. A decision to commit half her waking hours ... for several years ... to a relatively unknown entity ... is quite a life-impacting decision. While it varies person-to-person, she needs to reach a comfortable degree of certainty that the decision to accept your offer is the only reasonable choice.

You need to allay all her doubts, concerns, and fears. You should celebrate this amazing opportunity, what the organization will accomplish with her help, and who she will become along the way. In case it's not obvious, doing this via email alone is insufficient.

Throughout the courting process, as you've Screened and Evaluated this person, you and your team have learned so much about her past, her strengths, her weaknesses, her goals, her desires, and her dreams.

Even if she ultimately doesn't accept your offer, her experience will be memorable, leaving the door open for future employment opportunities or as a referral source for other A+ Talent.

🏆 ACHIEVEMENTS UNLOCKED

➢ Increase Offer Acceptance Rate
➢ Shorten Closing Stage Cycle Time
➢ Improve Employer Brand Quality

PART SIX

LOGISTICS

This section covers the mechanics of the overall Recruiting Process, as well as the craft inherit to designing a pleasant and highly engaging Candidate Experience.

The average position remained open for 44 Days in 2017, and companies reported an average cost of $500/day per position in lost business value. This means that shaving just a few days or a week off your average time-to-hire can produce tens of thousands in newly claimed value for your organization during even a moderately busy hiring period.

In addition to operating more efficiently, creating a great Candidate Experience is proven to increase your likelihood to hire the Candidates you want. According to a Glassdoor report, Organizations that invest in a strong candidate experience improve their quality of hires by 70%[10].

CREATE A WHITE-GLOVE PATH FOR TRUSTED REFERRALS

When receiving talent referrals from sources whose judgment you implicitly trust, resist the urge to send these Candidates through the same process you use for "organic" or "unvetted" Applicants. Fast track them to "the lightning round", go the extra mile on Candidate communication, etc.

Let's face it. Not all Candidates are created equal. The entire point of performing a rigorous Screening & Evaluation process is to ensure that you don't make an expensive and damaging hiring mistake on a mostly unknown entity. When a Candidate comes pre-vetted to some degree, however, there are segments of your Screening & Evaluation Stages that simply don't make sense, and pushing a pre-vetted Candidate through every segment wastes precious time, and it makes both the Candidate and the Referrer feel disenfranchised and undervalued for their efforts.

🏆 ACHIEVEMENTS UNLOCKED

➤ Shorten Overall Cycle Time
➤ Improve Candidate Experience
➤ Improve Internal Morale

STANDARDIZE YOUR INTERVIEW SCHEDULE

1. Once you have established a Bullpen of trusted Interviewers, survey them to determine 2-3 time slots each week they typically have availability, where each time slot meets or exceeds the length of a typical Interview.
2. Compile the responses, producing a predictable schedule of 5-10 potential holds to perform an Interview every week.
3. Communicate Interviewers' availability to the entire hiring team, ensuring proper coverage & extra Interviewer redundancy for each time slot.
4. Offer these time slots as options to a Candidate when scheduling an Interview.
5. Deviate from the standard schedule only when absolutely necessary.

This might have been the biggest time and focus savings I've ever accomplished for my Interviewer Bullpen as a Hiring Manager, and it's so simple I was kicking myself for not thinking of it years prior.

For every day of the week, I selected a pair of 2-hour time blocks, ensuring there would be Standard Interview times spanning anywhere from 8am through 6pm over the course of the calendar workweek.

Interviewers would select their best & preferred availability, and after just a handful of revisions, I could now provide Interviewers the most likely times they might be called to facilitate or participate in an Interview, with 90% predictability. This gives Candidates the impression that you're organized (and busy Evaluating other Candidates), and it significantly reduces the loss in productivity from team members who have to context switch between their primary responsibilities and "Interview Mode".

 ACHIEVEMENTS UNLOCKED

➢ Protect Interviewer Productivity
➢ Improve Internal Morale

LIMIT INTERVIEW FREQUENCY

Once you have a sense of who all needs to meet with a Candidate in order to perform a thorough Evaluation, schedule and conduct your Interviews in the least number of total days possible. Bias towards longer days of consecutive Interview sessions instead of shorter individual sessions spread over a number of days.

I know what you might be thinking: Marathon Interview days can be brutal and may turn a Candidates off. What would turn her off even more is having to take multiple partial days off from her current job, come up with multiple excuses as to why she needs the time off, and drive to your location 2, 3 or 4 separate times over a period of several weeks.

This can give the impression that you're disorganized and unprofessional, or that you just aren't very good at Evaluating Talent.

Also consider that during that time, she's considering other opportunities at other companies, and with each passing day you're lowering your chances she'll accept your offer, should you make one.

🏆 ACHIEVEMENTS UNLOCKED

➢ Improve Candidate Experience
➢ Shorten Evaluation Cycle Time
➢ Increase Offer Acceptance Rate

USE TEXT MESSAGES FOR QUICK COMMUNICATION

At an early point in the Sourcing or Screening Stages, request a Candidate's permission to allow you and/or the Recruiting team to communicate via text message in an effort to reduce or eliminate delays in guiding them through the process.

Millions (Billions?) of emails are overlooked or missed every day. The average text message response time is approximately 10 minutes. Enough said.

🏆 ACHIEVEMENTS UNLOCKED

➤ Improve Candidate Engagement
➤ Shorten Overall Cycle Time

COORDINATE VIA PHONE, NOT E-MAIL

When attempting to coordinate times for Phone Screens, Interviews and other critical Screening & Evaluation steps, mandate the use of synchronous communication with Candidates to reduce the amount of delay and churn between Employer and Candidate.

In our overly busy, smartphone-driven age, we have a tendency to choose the path that takes the least amount of time and effort without considering the impact of our chosen path.

And the biggest contributors to unnecessarily lengthy Recruiting Cycles without a doubt comes from dreaded "delay time" between segments in the Screening & Evaluation Stages. Countless days are wasted as Recruiting Coordinators and Candidates trade emails back-and-forth in an attempt to schedule phone screen or an in-person Interview. All it takes is a delay of ONE day for a high-value Candidate to decide to accept a competing offer.

As a general (life) rule of thumb: E-mail is great for announcements & communicating decisions, and it's ill-suited and utterly terrible as a conversational medium.

ACHIEVEMENTS UNLOCKED

➢ Improve Candidate Engagement

➢ Improve Candidate Experience

➢ Reduce Candidate Bleed Rate

MEASURE AND TRACK YOUR RESPONSE TIME

1. Schedule a meeting with Hiring Managers, Recruiters, and anyone else involved in decision-points and external communication for an open position.
2. At each stage where external communication occurs, agree upon a maximum turnaround time to communicate decisions and next steps to Candidates. These numbers will be known as your Service Level Agreement (SLA) for external communication for each Stage.
3. Using your Applicant Tracking System (ATS) or, in a pinch, e-mail, track and measure the team's adherence to your SLAs.

"What gets measured, gets managed."

While the adage is cliché, it's as true as it is commonplace. If there is no established standard to which your team agrees to adhere, you are implicitly admitting to having low standards.

Agreeing to communicate with Candidates within a handful of business days after each decision-point is not unreasonable, and publishing this standard even internally sets behavioral expectations for everyone involved in the process.

ACHIEVEMENTS UNLOCKED

➢ Shorten Overall Cycle Time

➢ Improve Candidate Experience

➢ Improve Employer Brand Quality

BE TRANSPARENT ABOUT "DELAY TIME" ACTIVITY

In communication with Prospects & Candidates, provide as much insight as possible not only about when they should expect to hear from you, but what's going on "behind the scenes" in the meantime.

If the team has already interviewed a candidate and is a "yes", but they'll be conducting Interviews with 4 other Candidates before making a decision? Tell her.

Are there delays in scheduling a Candidate's on-site Interview due to lack of Manager/Interviewer availability? Tell her.

Are you slightly altering the Position Profile due to recent changes in company goals or team composition? Well, you get the picture.

In looking to join a new organization, Applicants want to feel like they are a valued part of the Recruiting Process, not an infant that's spoon-fed only what you feel is good for them. The more opaque they feel you're being, the less engaged they become. A reasonable, high-quality A+ Talent has seen plenty of organizational shifts, delays and unforeseen obstacles in her time, and she will appreciate the refreshing candor that is typically hard to come by in conversations with a Hiring Team.

🏆 ACHIEVEMENTS UNLOCKED

- ➢ Improve Candidate Engagement
- ➢ Reduce Candidate Bleed Rate
- ➢ Improve Candidate Experience
- ➢ Improve Employer Branding Quality

IMPLEMENT SELF-SERVICE SCHEDULING

The proliferation of integrated scheduling apps like Calendly, Acuity Scheduling, Book Like a Boss etc. makes finding an agreeable meeting time easier than ever.

1. Create an account with one of these services
2. Integrate with the necessary Outlook/GSuite accounts in your organization (you may have to add multiple calendars)
3. Create and Configure Appointments for each type of interview in your Evaluation phase
4. Share the relevant URLs with candidates at each step of the Evaluation Phase.

It is staggering how frequently I've encountered situations where Recruiters or Coordinators spend days playing phone tag or trading e-mails with a candidate, trying to find the right day to schedule a phone screen or an interview. In just one day, you can lose a candidate to another offer or simply to disinterest & frustration.

If there's one thing that your candidate feels she doesn't have during the Evaluation process, it's control. Giving her control over something, while it may seem minor to you, will go a long way towards keeping her interested and engaged, while also saving you additional time and hassle.

 ACHIEVEMENTS UNLOCKED

> ➤ Improve Candidate Experience
> ➤ Shorten Evaluation Cycle Time
> ➤ Shorten Overall Cycle Time

CLEARLY COMMUNICATE NEXT STEPS AT EVERY STAGE

In your application process, e-mail communication, scheduling etc., always clearly state what a candidate can expect to happen next. Include:

- By when she should expect to hear from you
- How you will reach out (phone, e-mail, carrier pigeon)
- What the possible outcomes are (next evaluation stage, offer, end of the road)

There may be no business process more plagued by "ghosting" than the recruiting process. Trending Topics surface LinkedIn related to Recruiter ghosting or Candidate ghosting pretty much once a month. Because the bar is set so pathetically low, you can delight a candidate simply by telling her when you'll contact them next, and if things go well, what the next step will be.

Giving a candidate the certainty that there will be closure of some kind provides peace of mind, and it paints you as a more responsible and professional organization that treats candidates like human beings.

As a side benefit, behaving in a transparent fashion reduces the chance that you'll have a candidate go silent on you. Per the Reciprocation Principle, people want and expect interpersonal interactions to balance out, so a candidate is unlikely to ghost on you if she feels confident you wouldn't do it to her.

🏆 ACHIEVEMENTS UNLOCKED

- ➤ Improve Employer Brand Quality
- ➤ Improve Candidate Experience
- ➤ Enforce SLAs

CONSOLIDATE TALENT DATA INTO ONE SYSTEM

No matter the implementation, come to an agreement between Hiring Managers and your HR/Recruiting Team on "One Ring to Rule Them All". Import and consolidate all Recruiting workflows into a standard system.

All too often in small, growing organizations, each Hiring Manager uses his own preferred data store to track Leads, Prospects, Applicants, Candidates and Evaluation data. Once a Staff Recruiter is introduced into the mix, they are left juggling multiple disparate systems, trying to make sense of everything and "standardize" their practices with the digital equivalent of duct tape and bubblegum. Importing and consolidating into a single Applicant Tracking System (ATS) allows a single, easy-to-use solution for those who Administer your Recruiting Process, not to mention comparing and contrasting practices between Hiring Managers across different departments to share what works and what doesn't.

🏆 ACHIEVEMENTS UNLOCKED

➢ Reduce Recruiter/HR Administrative Churn
➢ Improve Metric Tracking & Benchmarking

REFERENCES

"2018 HIRED Global Brand Health Report" (PDF) 2018.
https://hired.com/brand-health-report

"50 HR and Recruiting Statistics for 2017: Statistical Reference Guide
for Recruiters" (PDF) 2017. https://resources.glassdoor.com/rs/899-
LOT-464/images/50hr-recruiting-and-statistics-2017.pdf

"Bloom's taxonomy". https://en.wikipedia.org/wiki/Bloom's_taxonomy

Bock, Laszlo. *Work Rules!: Insights from Inside Google That Will
Transform How You Live and Lead.* Twelve Publishing. 2015.

"Competencies Proficiency Scale". January 12, 2009. https://hr.nih.gov/
working-nih/competencies/competencies- proficiency-scale

"Dreyfus model of skill acquisition." https://en.wikipedia.org/wiki/
Dreyfus_ model_of_skill_acquisition

"Four stages of competence".

https://en.wikipedia.org/wiki/Four_stages_ of_competence

Perlis, Margaret M. Forbes. "8 Ways to Assess Leadership." Sep 16, 2012. https://www.forbes.com/sites/margaretperlis/2012/09/16/ inside-excellence-character-8-ways-to-assess-leadership-and-your-c andidates/

ACKNOWLEDGEMENTS

Ever since I was a child, I always knew I wanted to create things. I enjoyed drawing, up until I realized I couldn't draw faces. In 1994 I started building websites and teaching myself to code at age 12, even when I didn't have anything to create a website or program *about*. I also loved reading, and the creative writing portions of English class in middle- and high-school were extremely appealing. There was a part of me that always wanted to write a book, but back in the 90s that dream seemed impossible at worst and unlikely at best.

I want to thank my parents, Sue and Steve Martin, for always supporting me full-force in whatever extra-curricular activities I picked up. Whether it was piano, wrestling, baseball, or coding, they always took me to practices, cheered me on, and bought whatever we could afford to help me get better. I'll never forget the countless times they drove me to *Ollie's Discount Warehouse* and let me pick out 2 or 3 programming books that were an edition or two out of date, but to teenage me they were biblical in their nature.

I want to thank anyone who ever took a chance on hiring me as a web designer, webmaster, Systems Programmer, .Net Engineer, Dev Lead, Systems Architect, Sr Developer, Dev Manager or Director. Most of you took a chance on a selfish kid with dollar signs in his eyes who just wanted to code for a paycheck. All of you helped to develop a man with purpose and the hunger to improve the lives of as many professionals as I possibly can.

Lastly, I *must* thank you, dear reader, for taking a chance on some nerd's first book. Through each day, fighting an overactive brain that refused to focus, creating and revising the best content I could think of, loving this project one minute and hating it (and myself) the next, I considered giving up dozens of times. The single thing that kept me from throwing in the towel was you, the reader, and the ways this book might help you that I could never even fathom.

Thank you for reading my writing. I don't know if it's the meek writer or coder in me, but there will always be a part of me that doubts whether I've earned the privilege for anyone to give me the gift of their time in reading any of my work. I'm truly humbled and grateful.

Whether you loved the book or hated it, whether you'll keep it close by or use its pages to line the floor of a hamster-cage, I would love to hear your thoughts, which you can email to *books@rebase.cc*, and I promise to read your note personally.

ABOUT THE AUTHOR

Shaun P. Martin is a lifelong technologist who first taught himself to code at age 12, building websites for local & global companies before his 13th birthday. He eventually traded in his Engineer hat to tackle Management and Executive Leadership, becoming fascinated by the similarities between software and human systems.

Always an Entrepreneur at heart (his fifth grade teacher caught him selling cough drops and candy to classmates for a healthy profit) he founded Rebase, a company on a mission to eradicate outdated & ineffective Recruiting practices and help growing companies become a magnet for great talent.

www.ingramcontent.com/pod-product-compliance
Lightning Source LLC
Chambersburg PA
CBHW071314220526
45468CB00001B/372